MONSTER ⚙ MACHINES

TRUCKS

DAVID JEFFERIS

RAINTREE
STECK-VAUGHN
PUBLISHERS

A Harcourt Company

Austin   New York
www.steck-vaughn.com

▼ This eight-wheel truck was specially built for towing wrecked vehicles.

Library of Congress Cataloging-in-Publication Data
Jefferis, David.
    Trucks / David Jefferis.
    p. cm.—(Monster machines)
    Includes index.
    ISBN 0-7398-2879-7
    1. Trucks—Juvenile literature.
    [1. Trucks.] I. Title. II. Series.

TL230.15 .J44 2001
629.224—dc21

                      00-055246

Printed in Singapore
Bound in the United States
1 2 3 4 5 04 03 02 01 00

Acknowledgments
We wish to thank the following individuals and organizations for their help and assistance and for supplying material in their collections: Alpha Archive, Tim Andrew, Caterpillar Inc., George Hall/Code Red, DAF Racing, General Motors Corp., Kenworth Truck Company, Leyland Trucks, HW Lovell & Son, Leyland DAF, Monster Trucks.com, Oshkosh Truck Corp., Pakkar Inc., Peterbilt Motors Company, Quadrant Picture Library/Jeremy Hoare, Samsung Corp., Scania Trucks, Tamiya Inc., The Stock Market, Volvo Truck Corp.

Illustrations and diagrams by Ron Jobson, Gavin Page

CONTENTS

⚙ TECH TALK
Look for the cog and blue box for explanations of technical terms.

👁 EYE VIEW
Look for the eye and yellow box for eyewitness accounts.

HEAVY HAULERS

Trucks haul most of the world's freight. They carry goods on roads that range from mountain tracks to superhighways.

▲ In 1911 most trucks were built with cabs that were open to wind and weather.

Trucks are made in two basic types. Rigid trucks have a single metal backbone, called the chassis. The cab, engine, and wheels are mounted on the chassis. Cargo is carried behind the cab.

rigid truck   *semitrailer*

▼ Here you can see the chassis of a rigid truck. The engine sits under the cab. Rigid trucks are mostly light- or medium-weight designs.

cab

chassis

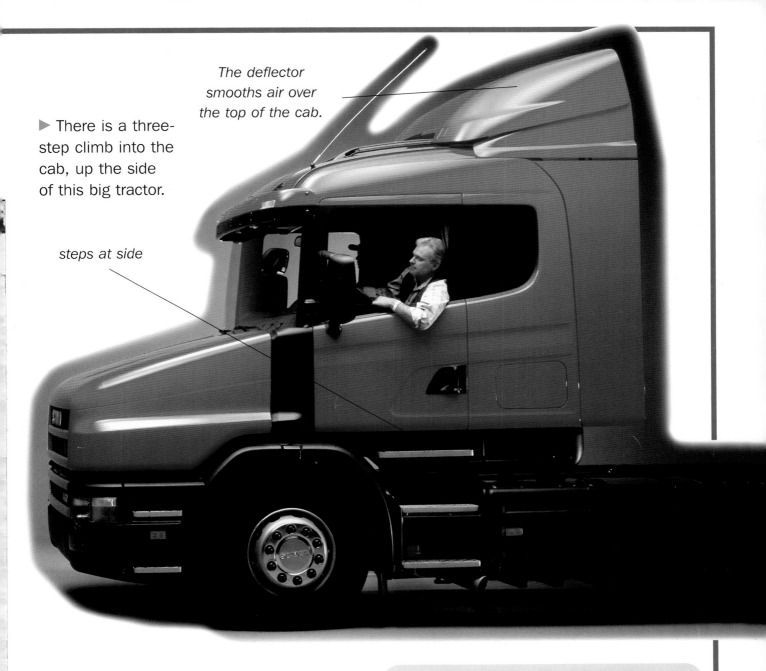

The deflector smooths air over the top of the cab.

▶ There is a three-step climb into the cab, up the side of this big tractor.

steps at side

Semitrailers ("semis") are made in two parts. In the front there is a tractor, with a powerful engine and a cab. The tractor tows the trailer, which carries the load.

Semis are used to haul big loads. A good driver can squeeze even a large semi into tight spots for loading or unloading.

⚙ EARLY STEAM POWER

The first trucks were steam-powered. Today trucks use diesel engines. Maurice LeBlanc's steam van of 1892 had a crew of two. The driver steered the van, while a stoker at the back shoveled coal into a furnace. Diesel trucks are easier to use and quicker.

POWER CENTER

Almost all trucks are powered by diesel engines. These are tough, long-lasting, and use less fuel than gas engines.

▲ Truckers admire a new truck during a stop for refueling.

A truck diesel engine is big and heavy. It may weigh about 1,100 pounds (500 kg). This is about the same as seven grown men. Such an engine is powerful enough to drive a 40-ton truck at 62 miles per hour (100 kph) or more.

Old or badly serviced diesels can give out smelly black exhaust fumes. The newest designs are much cleaner than this.

▲ Trucks with diesel engines can pull heavy loads at low speeds.

The radiator sucks air in to cool the engine.

The engine has about a thousand parts.

▲ The powerful diesel engine is the heart of a truck.

Usually the engine is hidden below a truck's cab. The picture here shows a new engine, before it goes into a truck.

The diesel engine is a complex piece of equipment, but it is tough and long-lasting. Most diesels give many years of reliable service.

⚙ **MOON TRUCKING**
A working truck may cover 500,000 miles (800,000 km) or more before being scrapped. This is about the same distance as driving to the Moon and back! Many parts in both engine and truck will be repaired or replaced during this time, from tires to windshield wipers.

BIG RIGS

Big rig is the nickname for the huge trucks that speed along the world's major highways.

▲ This rig can cruise at 75 mph (120 kph).

▼ A bug screen at the front of this rig helps keep the windshield free of insects.

bug screen

fuel tank at either side

KENWORTH

R·8037

◉ CRASH TESTING

"New trucks are designed with safety in mind. We set up a test truck to hit a concrete block at high speed. The results are checked to make sure the safety equipment works. A dummy driver sits in the cab....The noise when the truck hits the block is *unbelievable!*"

Technician at test area

▲ New trucks have big, soft air bags in the cab that protect drivers in a crash.

trailer, or the load-carrying part of the rig

A big rig's rear section is called the trailer. It hooks onto the back of the tractor and can be unhooked at the end of a trip. Then, it is unloaded. The trucker can quickly attach a newly filled trailer. This saves time, because the new load can be taken right away.

All kinds of things are hauled by truck. The rig pictured on the left is carrying fresh fish. These are kept cold by a refrigerator. Cooling equipment is very important for loads that will spoil if they get warm. Without it, this truck's fish would soon begin to smell.

LONG-DISTANCE TRUCKING

Many big-rig truckers travel about 100,000 miles (160,000 km) a year. For truckers, this is just part of the job.

▲ This trucker takes a break on a long haul in Arizona.

On long runs, many truckers use sleeper cabs. If they use their rig as a mobile home, thieves cannot steal the truck or its load in the night. Sleeper rigs can be very comfortable. Bunk beds, dressers, stereos, and microwave ovens are among the many things that sleeper rigs can have inside.

▶ The Kenworth T2000 sleeper cab is like a small caravan.

👁 TAKING A BREAK

"My sleeper cab may be compact. But, in many ways, it's cozier than my real home! I have a small refrigerator for food, and a microwave reheats meals quickly. I can watch color TV, and I have a paperback mini-library. I use the cell phone to call my wife and children. Sometimes I play games on my laptop computer to relax before going to sleep. My favorite is a flight-simulator game. Maybe I should have been a fighter-jet pilot!" *Long-distance trucker*

10

▲ Dockside cranes lift cargo from a ship. The cargo is then taken to its destination by truck.

Truckers in Europe may drive through several countries in a day. For example, it is possible to cross Belgium in less than three hours.

▶ Instruments in the cab keep drivers up-to-date with how a truck is running. Fuel and oil levels are among the many things shown.

ROAD TRAIN

Road trains are used only in Australia. A road train is made up of a powerful tractor, towing a line of two, three, or more trailers behind.

▲ This megarig tows three tankers and has 62 wheels.

Australia's hot desert center, the Outback, is where you can see most road trains. There, truckers haul loads of 100 tons or more over long distances.

A fuel stop takes some time, because trucks have to fill up with 130 gallons (500 l) or more of diesel oil. A truck can drive for about 750 miles (1,200 km) before the fuel tanks need a refill.

▼ Drivers take a break in the heat of the Australian sun.

► Truck cabs are filled with controls. Air conditioning is used to keep the cab cool.

The gauge shows the engine's speed.

The power steering system makes turning the wheel easier.

A road train crossing the Outback is quite a sight. You can see dust thrown up by the wheels from miles away. If you are near the truck as it hurtles by, you can be choked by a mini dust storm. It's best to stay clear.

Kangaroos should keep away, too. Many are killed because they do not hop aside.

Many kangaroos are hit by speeding trucks.

parked semitrailers

✪ MELTING TIRES

It is so hot in the deserts of Australia's "red center" that truckers have to keep their speed down, so that the tires don't melt. At noon, temperatures may be more than 104°F (40°C), so truckers drive at about 40 mph (70 kph). At night, when it is cooler, trucks can go faster.

TANKERS

▲ This tanker carries oil. The driver has to be very careful, because oil can catch fire easily.

Tanker trucks haul many kinds of liquids. Some liquids are easy to carry. Others need special care.

Liquids such as milk or water are easy to carry. They pour well and can easily be pumped in and out of a tanker. Fats have to be heated, since they become solid when cold. Very cold liquids are kept cool with powerful refrigerators.

▲ It takes only a few minutes to pump 260 gallons (1,000 l) of oil.

▶ This liquid oxygen tanker stores its load at a very chilly –297°F (–183°C).

⚙ SLOSHING AROUND

No trucker wants a shifting load. This affects a truck's balance, which makes turning corners dangerous. To help, tanks are built with stiff metal blades inside that slow down liquid when it swirls around. Tanks often have several small compartments, since sloshing in each of these is less than in one big tank.

▶ Ready-mixed concrete has to be kept turning so that it does not set hard before it arrives at a building site.

The tanker's body is made of special material to help keep the load cold.

SHIFTING THE DIRT

The building industry uses trucks to haul away dirt before the building work begins.

Dump trucks are among the most useful heavy trucks. They have huge tires and are super strong. This means that they can take the knocks and bangs of tough work. Bigger trucks are often made of solid steel 1 inch (2.5 cm) thick.

Builders usually have to work in a hurry, so speed is important. For all its size, a dump truck like the one below can roar along at 30 miles per hour (50 kph) or more.

▲ This dump truck can carry 20 tons of dirt at a time.

▶ A dump truck is loaded by a digger-excavator.

A power shovel loads three tons of rock at a time.

Power-assisted controls make the excavator easy to handle.

⚙ DUCKWALKING

This dump truck is a "frame-steer" design. It has a joint behind the cab. This lets the driver steer by twisting the entire front half of the truck from side to side, rather than just turning the front wheels. At slow speeds, frame-steer trucks wiggle as they steer. Drivers call it duckwalking!

MEGATRUCK!

The world's heaviest trucks are used in the mining industry for carrying huge loads of rock and earth.

Home for these large trucks is in such places as the huge copper mines of Zaire, in Africa. There dump trucks are driven around the clock. Each one shifts thousands of tons of rock every day.

The biggest truck of all is the Caterpillar Model 797. Fully loaded, the big Cat weighs about 600 tons, more than half of which is a big mound of dirt. The dirt weighs about the same as a pile of 300 cars.

It may be big, but the 797 is easy to drive. This is because the controls are power-assisted.

▲ The Cat 797 can speed along at 40 mph (64 kph).

👁 IN CHARGE OF A TRUCKING GIANT

"In the cab, my eye line is over 20 feet (6 m) above the ground, so I get a great all-around view. The seat is comfy, with air springs. These are needed for long hours at the wheel. Controls are power-assisted, which means you don't need too much muscle. But climbing to and from the cab several times a day helps keep me fit!" *Dumper driver*

▼ Mining machines lead a tough life, as you can see from the dents in the thick steel bodywork of this dumper.

FIREFIGHTERS

Fire trucks range from pumpers built to drench a fire, to extending-ladder trucks.

▲ The 1899 Merryweather fire engine used a steam engine for pumping water.

For fires in buildings, fire crews pump thousands of gallons of water to drown flames. Once the fire is under control, dry powder can be sprayed on areas that are still hot.

In an aircraft or vehicle crash, burning fuel is the main danger. So fire crews spray foam at the fire. Water in the foam cools things down, and special gas in the bubbles smothers the flames.

▶ A ladder truck arrives at a blaze. The crew will soon raise the ladder to reach the fire.

firefighting platform

✿ UP ON A LADDER

Firefighters often have to reach the upper floors of buildings, where people might be trapped in a blaze. The extending ladder on this fire truck has a top platform to make rescues easier. There are movement controls on the platform, as well as down on the truck.

SAN JOSE FIRE DEPT

► Fire crews have to train so they are ready for any emergency. Here, an airfield crash truck sprays foam on an old airliner, used for practice.

Foam is pumped onto the fire.

A ladder can be raised and turned on the truck's turntable.

8180   70   60   50   40

AN JOSE FIRE DEPT.   BREATHING AIR

LIGHT TRUCKS

▲ Radio-controlled monster trucks are quite popular. This one is 12 inches (30 cm) long.

Light trucks are very popular. They are short and thick, and can carry big loads when needed.

Many light trucks have a four-wheel drive system, in which power from the engine goes to all the wheels. Four-wheel drive is useful for driving across rough country or in slippery mud. With all four wheels turning, you can keep going in places where a two-wheel drive truck would get stuck.

◄ This pickup truck has a four-wheel drive system.

⚙ DRIVING THE WHEELS

In most trucks and cars, the engine drives two wheels, either at the back or the front. On a slippery surface, it's easy for these two wheels to lose grip and spin around and around, until the vehicle stops. Four-wheel drive adds a pair of powered wheels to give extra grip.

► The Hummer was first built as an army truck. Lots of pop stars and movie actors wanted one, so the maker made a version for them, too.

▲ Pick-up trucks with giant tires and big engines perform as "monster trucks" at shows. Often they crush cars as a favorite act!

The engine is above the waterline.

👁 UNDERWATER TRUCKING

"We teach off-road driving skills. Our obstacle course has a muddy lake, through which you drive. You must go at the right speed—not so slow that the wheels lose grip, not so fast that water splashes over the front. If the engine drowns, the vehicle will stop. Then we make the driver wade through the mud to fetch a rescue cable!" *Course tutor*

FUTURE TRUCKS

Designers are busy working on trucks that will create little pollution and use less fuel. Making trucks quieter and safer is important, too.

Oily, black diesel exhaust fumes could soon be a thing of the past. New engines burn their fuel better, so they are cleaner than the earlier designs. Natural gas is another kind of fuel. It is already used by some trucks. It burns very cleanly, so it is very important for trucks that are going to be used in cities.

▲ This present-day truck runs on natural gas. This is a fuel that creates much less pollution when it is burned than diesel oil.

▶ This is one idea for a future truck. The body panels would be made of aluminum, a metal that does not rust.

⚙ BURNING NEW FUELS

Diesel oil is the standard truck fuel, and is likely to remain so, at least for the time being. Present-day diesels are cleaner than old types, and future designs will be even better. In the future, more trucks may use natural gas, which is cleaner than any diesel being planned. Hydrogen gas may also be used. Its waste gas is just steam, made of pure water.

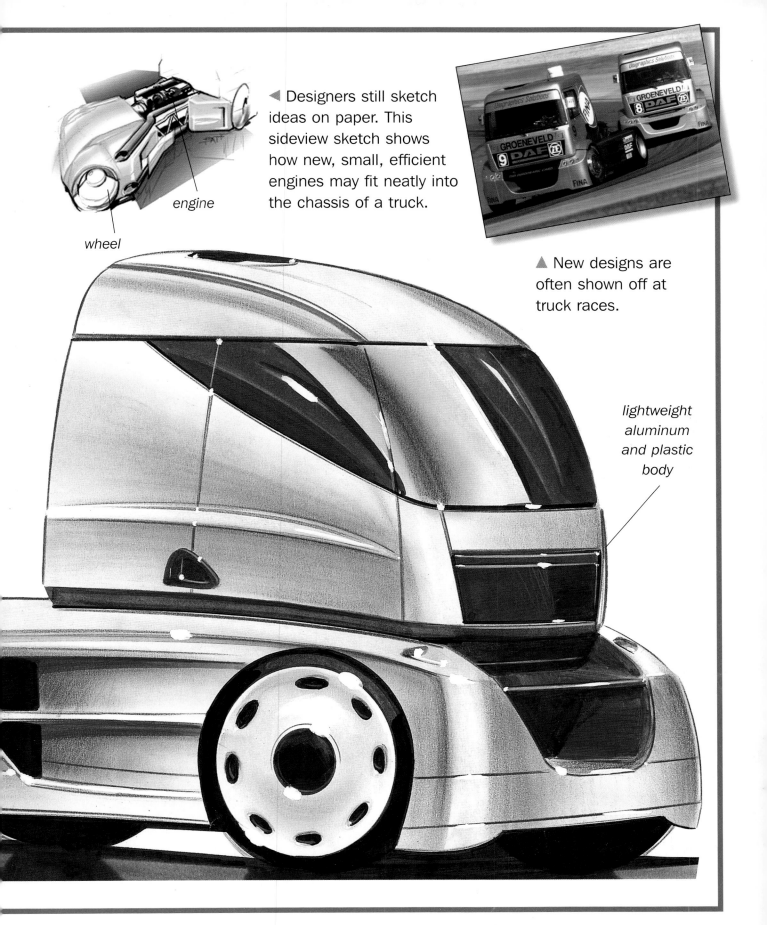

◄ Designers still sketch ideas on paper. This sideview sketch shows how new, small, efficient engines may fit neatly into the chassis of a truck.

engine

wheel

▲ New designs are often shown off at truck races.

lightweight aluminum and plastic body

▼ Cugnot's steam truck, towing a cannon

TRUCK FACTS

Here are some facts from the world of trucks and trucking.

Steam truck

The first truck was made by Nicholas Cugnot, in 1769. The steam-powered three-wheeler was built to haul guns for the French Army. A second model was built, and this could pull a four-ton load, but only at walking pace.

Bulldog strength

The Mack company's trucks were called "bulldogs" by soldiers for their strength and reliability in the army. Mack adopted the bulldog as its company symbol.

Mountain crossing

Truckers risk their lives when driving through the Himalaya Mountains, between India and China. The roads are so bad that drivers often have to creep slowly along narrow tracks that wind along the sides of mountains. In the valleys far below lie the rusting wrecks of trucks that didn't stay on the road.

Saving fuel

A big rig uses about .25 gallons (1 l) of fuel every 2 miles (3 km). Fuel costs money, so drivers use every trick they know to save fuel. Even parking on a flat road to avoid an uphill start makes a small difference.

Computer truck

The Renault Magnum has a built-in electronic "doctor," which checks on how the truck is performing. You can plug in a laptop computer to see the amount of fuel used or distance traveled.

◄ Mack trucks have a shiny bulldog above the radiator grille.

Nonstop dumper

Giant mining dumpers are worked far harder than their drivers. Most dumpers are used 16 hours a day, with three or four changes of driver during that time. One record-breaking dumper beat this by working over 56 minutes an hour, every single day, for a year. The only time out was for refueling and for servicing.

Race to the clouds

Every year truckers roar up the 14,250-foot (4,343-m) high Pikes Peak in Colorado, in a race to be quickest to the top. Back in 1901, when Pikes Peak racing started, it took over nine hours to get up. Today cars manage the run in just 10 minutes, and trucks are not far behind. The 1999 trucking king was Mike Ryan, who blasted to the top in just over 15 minutes. Ryan is actually a stunt driver. In the same year, he jumped a truck over 65 feet (20 m) through the air, while it was on fire!

▲ Dumper truck used for hauling rock from a mine

Tachograph time

European drivers have a '"spy" in the cab called a tachograph. This notes the time and distance traveled. The tacho is a safety device, made to keep truckers from driving too long at one time. A tired driver can make a mistake and cause an accident.

Custom trucks

Customizing is a popular way to mark your truck. Some people just add a name to the cab door, or maybe a stripe or two. Others go further, with gleaming new paint, chromed parts, leather seats and sleeper cabs with luxury fittings.

Muddy drive

In 1999 truckers taking food aid to refugees in Albania had to use roads that were often just long mud holes. At times it took an hour to slither along a 3-mile (5km) stretch.

▼ Customized show truck

TRUCK WORDS

Here are some of the technical terms used in this book.

▲ Cabover truck

Air bag
A safety device stored inside the center of a steering wheel. In a crash, it blows up to act as a cushion to protect the driver. Some trucks have a second air bag to protect a passenger.

Big rig
The name for the combination of tractor and semitrailer used for hauling big loads.

Cab-over
A truck design that sits the cab on top of the engine. The cab tilts over, so an engineer can reach the engine when it needs servicing. A regular truck design has the engine under a long hood in front of the driver.

Chassis
(CHA-see)
The strong metal structure to which truck parts (such as engine and wheels) are attached.

Diesel engine
(DEE-zuhl EN-jin)
The type of engine used in most trucks. It was invented by the German Otto Diesel in the 19th century. It burns special oil and is efficient, but quite noisy, compared to a gas engine.

Four-wheel drive
Vehicle with engine power that drives all four wheels. In "wheel code" this is known as a 4 x 4.

Frame-steer
A semitrailer that is steered by twisting the tractor unit from side to side, rather

Inside a diesel engine

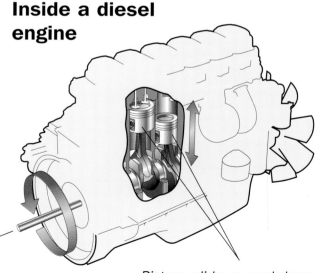

shaft turns wheels

Pistons slide up and down. Inside cylinders turn a shaft.

than steering with the front wheels. These wheels roll forward or back, but do not change direction for steering.

Rigid
(RI-jid)
A truck with a single steel chassis, on which the cab and load area are mounted. Semitrailers are split into two sections, with the tractor in front. This pulls the load-carrying sections.

Road train
A big Australian rig, often with three or more trailers. Road trains haul loads across the vast outback, Australia's hot desert center.

▲ A mobile digger loads a rigid-chassis dumper truck.

Semitrailer
(sem-eye-TRAY-ler)
A type of trailer used with artic rigs. It can be hitched and unhitched to a tractor in a few minutes.

Sleeper cab
A cab with its own built-in sleeping area. Most have a bunk bed, a small wardrobe, a TV, and other comforts.

Tachograph
(TACK-o-graf)
A machine fitted to European trucks. It shows the time and distance traveled. Drivers in tacho-equipped trucks must take breaks at set times to avoid tiredness.

◄ The arrow shows one of this tanker semi's front support legs.

TRUCK PROJECTS

These easy experiments show you some of the science behind the world of trucks and trucking.

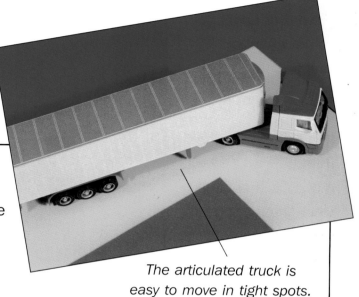

BENDING AROUND CORNERS

Semitrailers or semis are used for a very good reason—they are much easier to drive around tight corners. Try parking a model truck to see the difference having a separate truck and trailer makes.

The articulated truck is easy to move in tight spots.

SPREADING THE WEIGHT

Big trucks have many wheels to avoid sinking into soft ground or breaking highway surfaces. For this experiment you need flour, a container, toy blocks, and a 16-ounce (450-g) can of beans.

1. Pour the flour into the container. You need a depth of about 1 inch (3 cm). Level the surface with a flat-edged kitchen utensil, such as a plastic spatula.

2. Next, build a simple truck shape from the toy blocks. Use a platform section, with two narrow blocks at each end. These do the job of wheels.

cooler
fitted on
front of
trailer

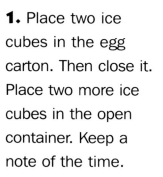

KEEPING LOADS COOL

Refrigeration units can keep a load cool, but good insulation is needed also. For this experiment you need a plastic egg carton, a small container, and four ice cubes. Time your experiment with an accurate watch.

1. Place two ice cubes in the egg carton. Then close it. Place two more ice cubes in the open container. Keep a note of the time.

2. After 20 minutes, the open ice cubes (arrowed) should be melting. Now check the egg carton. The cubes there should still be frozen.

3. Build a second unit, but have double-width blocks at the ends. This double width should do the same job as the extra tires on a full-sized truck.

4. Place the first block unit on the flour. Gently place the can of beans on top. Be ready to catch the can if it falls sideways. When the blocks have sunk in, carefully lift the can off, and place it to one side. Gently lift the block unit out of the flour.

5. Measure how far the blocks have sunk in. Now smooth the flour, and repeat with the double-width blocks. You should find this unit hardly sinks in at all.

INDEX